DEDICATION

I would like to dedicate this book to the memory of Don Thompson. Don passed away whilst this volume was being prepared for publication; many *Tramway Classics* books have included his superb photographic work. It is particularly fitting that the area covered by Barnet and Finchley Tramways was Don's home territory.

Published April 1997

ISBN 1 873793 93 6

© Middleton Press 1997

Design - Deborah Goodridge

Published by Middleton Press
Easebourne Lane
Midhurst
West Sussex
GU29 9AZ
Tel: 01730 813169
Fax: 01730 812601

Printed & bound by Biddles Ltd,
Guildford and Kings Lynn

CONTENTS

INTRODUCTION AND ACKNOWLEDGEMENTS

Tramways have always held a particular fascination and in this volume of the *Tramway Classics* series I have endeavoured to bring to life some of the day-to-day scenes of a bygone age. Although the trams depicted in these pages belong to the past, the wheel has now turned full circle and, at the time of writing, construction has started south of the Thames on a new tramway system for Croydon. Perhaps it is not too much to hope, that in the near future the citizens of Finchley and Barnet will have access to modern, pollution free light rail vehicles which will enhance the quality of public transport.

My thanks go to the following who have made contributions to the text and pictures: C.Carter, R.S.Carpenter, John Gent, John Gillham, Dave Jones, John Meredith, A.D.Packer, J.A.Pullen, the National Tramway Museum for views from the collections of H.B.Priestley and D.W.K.Jones, the London Transport Museum for permission to use LT traffic circulars, timetables and the official MET views, Sara Leitch for the use of photos from her late father, Dr.Hugh Nicol, Ann Watkins for material from her late husband, Alan Watkins, and a special vote of thanks to B.J. "Curly" Cross for allowing me to peruse his vast collection of tramway material. My sincere apologies go to anyone whose name I have missed; some views included in this book do not have any indication of the photographer's name, and despite enquiries, I have been unable to locate this information.

Preparation of detailed car plans has again been undertaken by Terry Russell to whom I am very grateful. Finally, those seeking more information are directed to the two volume work on the MET written by Cyril Smeeton, and to companion *Tramway Classics* volumes by Dave Jones.

GEOGRAPHICAL SETTING

The landscape north of London is hilly and was once part of the counties of Hertfordshire, Middlesex and London. On the formation of Greater London in April 1965, the new Borough of Barnet was extended to take in Finchley and Golders Green. Archway Road is now divided between Haringey and Islington.

The maps used in this book are from the Ordnance Survey 1914 and 1936 editions to a scale of 25ins. to the foot (1:2500).

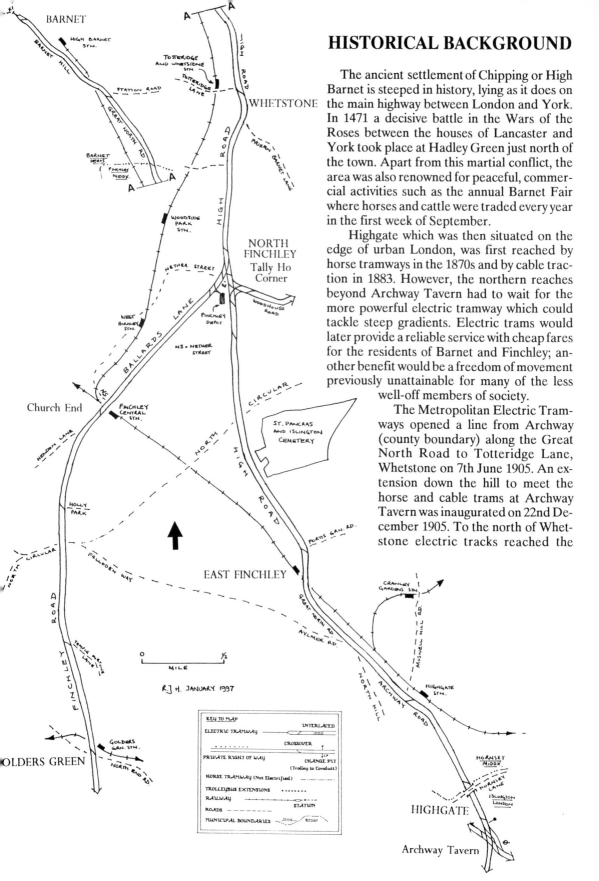

HISTORICAL BACKGROUND

The ancient settlement of Chipping or High Barnet is steeped in history, lying as it does on the main highway between London and York. In 1471 a decisive battle in the Wars of the Roses between the houses of Lancaster and York took place at Hadley Green just north of the town. Apart from this martial conflict, the area was also renowned for peaceful, commercial activities such as the annual Barnet Fair where horses and cattle were traded every year in the first week of September.

Highgate which was then situated on the edge of urban London, was first reached by horse tramways in the 1870s and by cable traction in 1883. However, the northern reaches beyond Archway Tavern had to wait for the more powerful electric tramway which could tackle steep gradients. Electric trams would later provide a reliable service with cheap fares for the residents of Barnet and Finchley; another benefit would be a freedom of movement previously unattainable for many of the less well-off members of society.

The Metropolitan Electric Tramways opened a line from Archway (county boundary) along the Great North Road to Totteridge Lane, Whetstone on 7th June 1905. An extension down the hill to meet the horse and cable trams at Archway Tavern was inaugurated on 22nd December 1905. To the north of Whetstone electric tracks reached the

Middlesex/Hertfordshire boundary on 4th August 1906 and finally the market town of Barnet on 28th March 1907. Meanwhile, rails were advancing from Wood Green through New Southgate to Finchley, and this section opened on 8th April 1909. Golders Green was connected to Finchley on 16th December 1909, with the service being further extended on 21st February 1910 to Cricklewood, thereby linking up with the MET's western section. Large numbers of passengers were thus able to change from tram to underground train at Golders Green Station which had been opened by the Charing Cross, Euston and Hampstead Railway in June 1907.

Further connections with the metropolis appeared in the shape of joint services with the London County Council, and by the end of 1913 the following routes were operated:

21	*Holborn - Wood Green -*
	North Finchley (LCC/MET joint)
34	*Wood Green - North Finchley*
36	*Highgate - North Finchley*
38	*Highgate - North Finchley - Barnet*
40	*Cricklewood - Golders Green -*
	North Finchley
42	*Cricklewood - Golders Green -*
	Whetstone (Totteridge Lane)
44	*Cricklewood - Golders Green - Barnet*
46	*Golders Green - North Finchley*

On 24th September 1914 a new change pit was installed outside the Archway Tavern, this enabled trams to operate through services over the LCC conduit lines. MET services 36 and 38 were replaced by service 9 from Moorgate to Barnet (operated by LCC cars) and service 19 from Tottenham Court Road to Tally Ho Corner, Finchley (operated by MET cars).

The 1920s marked steady progress on the tramways with the introduction of faster vehicles, and in 1927 there appeared Bluebell, the first of a number of experimental tramcars which culminated in the famous Feltham design. Inspite of this modernisation the storm clouds were gathering and on 1st July 1933 London Transport came into existence. It was soon apparent that the tramcar was out of favour, as was proved when the new board drew up plans for trolleybus conversion of railbound routes. The lines west of Tally Ho Corner perished on 2nd August 1936, to be followed by the final disappearance of trams in the area on 6th March 1938. Finchley Depot was converted to serve the new trolleybuses. The era of electric street traction finally ended in 1961/2 when the local trolleybuses were ousted by diesel buses.

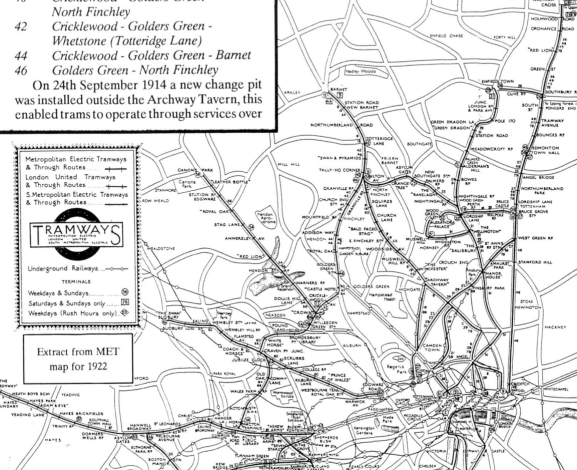

Extract from MET map for 1922

BARNET

1.   We begin our journey at Barnet Church tram terminus. A line of passengers is about to descend from the top deck of MET type C car 163. In this pre-First World War view we can also note above the headlamp the white disc with red circle and letter B indicator of the Highgate - Barnet service. This was before the introduction of route numbers. (D.Jones Coll.)

2.   The photographer now surveys the scene from an upstairs window of a neighbouring building. The camera looks down on car 121 in the first week of tramways in Barnet - March/April 1907. This vehicle is a type A and has a Robinson split staircase.   (B.J.Cross Coll.)

3.   Car 129 will begin its journey in Hertfordshire, then cross Middlesex to arrive in Highgate, County of London. This postcard was franked 30th March 1907 only two days after the official opening. As was often the case in the first decade of the twentieth century, the new mechanical marvel has attracted a crowd of very interested children. No doubt, they will soon part with the odd "copper" for a ride down Barnet Hill and out into the big world! (R.J.Harley Coll.)

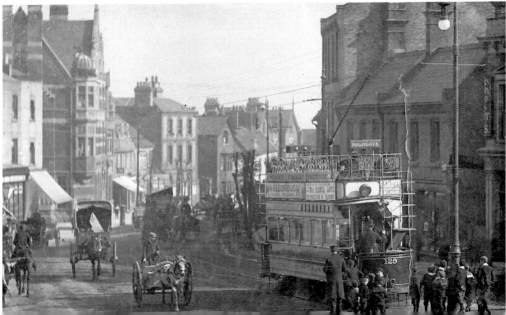

4.   A fine summer's day and what could be better than a trip on the top deck of car 116. Other folks are more intent on cycling to their destinations. The broom by the tram indicates that a spot of car cleaning may have just taken place.   (J.B.Gent Coll.)

5.   There are less people about in this view which may have been taken on a Sunday or a bank holiday. The motorman by car 111 waits until the photographer has finished. (R.J.Harley Coll.)

6.   The Cross of St.George flies high above as car 234 prepares to depart on service 36. Time has moved on from the last photo and the tree outside St.John's has been felled.
(J.B.Gent Coll.)

Barnet 1914

7. An attractive combination of ecclesiastical architecture and the pleasant lines of a former Metropolitan Electric tramcar greet the traveller as the sun sets on Barnet. During the First World War a specially adapted tramcar, which had been fitted with a searchlight on the top deck, was stationed on this terminal stub. Normal service cars were then obliged to reverse at the crossover just back from the terminus. (R.J.Harley Coll.)

8. Wednesday, 12th May 1937 was the coronation day of King George VI. Car 2224 (ex-MET car 292) bears red/blue circular markings to indicate a special working to Tottenham Court Road. The first trams to reach terminals bordering the central London vehicular traffic exclusion zone started to arrive from 4am on Coronation Day. Anybody wanting to take a bus on this auspicious occasion would have been unlucky - the drivers and conductors were all on strike! (D.W.K.Jones)

455.—BARNET STATION STOP BY REQUEST—POLE 297 BARNET HILL.

Notice to Motormen—Finchley Depot.

This stop has recently been made a *Head* stop and must be strictly observed as such so as to avoid any part of the car when stationary fouling the Pedestrian Crossing.

9. New overhead is already in place as car 2201 passes near High Barnet Station. The tram is drawing power from the positive charged trolleybus wire. (B.J.Cross Coll.)

←——————

10. Disaster came to Barnet Hill on 17th June 1927 when motorman Maurice Kent lost his life. Car 318 which he was driving, collided with the rear of a Scammell lorry stopped by road-works on the south side of Station Approach. This photo shows the wreckage before the tram was towed back to Finchley Depot. Car 318's subsequent history is covered in the Rolling Stock section. (D.Jones Coll.)

11. The semaphore signal on the former LNER High Barnet branch - part of the Northern Line from April 1940 - stands at danger as car 2275 passes underneath the bridge. In a few days service 19 will cease to exist and this stretch of road will be the preserve of the 609 trolleybus. Tram service 19 had no direct trolleybus replacement. Another detail to be noted here is the closely spaced tracks which precluded the operation of Felthams between Whetstone and Barnet. (D.W.K.Jones)

1935 timetable for service 19

19	BARNET — HIGHGATE — TOTTENHAM CT. RD.	MON. to FRI.		SATURDAY		SUNDAY	
		First	Last	First	Last	First	Last
	Via Gt. North Road, Whetstone, North Finchley, East Finchley, Archway Road, Junction Road, Kentish Town, Camden Town, Camden Road, Hampstead Road. Service Interval 6—8 mins. Journey time, 54 mins. Through fare 8d.	Barnet to N Finchley (Tally Ho Corner)	5 51 6 8 12 0	5 51 6 8 12 0	9 11 11 41
		Barnet to Tottenham Court Road............	5 51 6 8 11 44	5 51 6 8 11 45	9 11 10 54
		Tally Ho Corner to Tottenham Court Road....	4 25 4 46 11 59	4 25 4 46 12 0	8 8 11 9
		Tally Ho Corner to Highgate	4 25 4 46 12 4	4 25 4 46 12 4	7 37 11 9
	* LATER CAR : 11.36 to Whetstone.	Tottenham Court Road to Barnet............	5 11 5 25 11 4	5 11 5 25 11* 4	8 48 10†47
	† LATER CAR : 10.55 to Whetstone.	Tottenham Ct. Rd. to Tally Ho Corner......	5 11 5 25 12 40	5 11 5 25 12 41	8 48 11 48
		Highgate to Barnet......	5 30 5 45 11 23	5 30 5 45 11 23	9 6 11 5
		Highgate to Tally Ho Corner................	5 30 5 45 12 59	5 30 5 45 12 59	8 0 11 6
		Tally Ho Corner to Barnet................	5 35 5 50 11 43	5 35 5 50 11 43	8 54 11 25

12. This is the first of a trio of views taken near Lyonsdown Road north of Whetstone. Here we observe car 2214 (ex-MET type H car 282) near the Hertfordshire/Middlesex county boundary. In those days "air conditioning" meant lowering the top deck windows when the weather was rather warm! (D.W.K.Jones)

13. Car 881 which also appears on the cover of this book, is now in LT livery, but still retains its open platforms. Maybe this is the reason why the motorman is wearing his heavy winter coat and gauntlets, however, they present somewhat of a contrast with the sunglasses and white topped summer cap! The Moorgate - Barnet service 9 was replaced on 6th March 1938 by trolleybus route 609, which in turn gave way to bus route 104 on 8th November 1961. (D.W.K.Jones)

14. Our final view in this section is of car 2188 which shows clearly by the front bulkhead the white Metropolitan Stage Carriage licence no. 1780. Tramcars, buses and cabs were all licensed by the Metropolitan Police and this white plate was carried at one end of the car only. On the rocker panel is the REVISED STOPPING PLACES notice issued by LT to inform passengers of changes to the location of stop signs along the route. (D.W.K.Jones)

15. An early shot of car 103 shows the conductor leaning out from the top deck to check that all are safely aboard. The tram has practically the whole of the main road to itself. (B.J.Cross Coll.)

16. Outside Whetstone Post Office by the Griffin Inn stands an interesting array of street furniture which includes a drinking trough for thirsty horses. On the highway a line of centre poles frames MET type A car 101 as it halts to take on passengers. (R.J.Harley Coll.)

17. Car 1149 reverses on the last day, 5th March 1938. The conductor dutifully swings the pole as a couple of passengers disembark. From tomorrow the replacing single ended, six wheel trolleybuses will not be able to perform a simple reversal in the middle of the main road. They will normally require a complete turning loop to get back to where they came from. (D.Jones Coll.)

More details of the replacing Trolleybus services can be found on the next page.

Whetstone 1914

18. A tram passes the Griffin Inn, Whetstone. The village atmosphere is enhanced by the roof line of the various shops and houses. This shows the charm of English vernacular architecture at its most distinctive. (R.J.Harley Coll.)

1732.—TROLLEYBUS CONVERSION—HOLLOWAY AND FINCHLEY DEPOTS AND OTHER ROUTE ALTERATIONS.

Notice to Inspectors and Conductors—Edmonton, Finchley, Hackney, Hampstead, Hendon, Holloway, Poplar, Stamford Hill, Stonebridge, Wood Green, Camberwell and Norwood Depots.

Commencing on Sunday, 6th March, 1938, the following route alterations will become effective :—

1. Conversions to Trolleybus operation.

Existing Tram Route	New Trolleybus Route		Remarks
	Number	Between	
17	**517/617** (Holloway Depot)	North Finchley Terminus and Holborn/ Farringdon Street Loop via Highgate	Routes running to London via Grays Inn Road will show 517 or 521 and will retain these numbers back to the Suburban Terminus. Routes to London via Farringdon Road will show 617 or 621 and retain these numbers back to the Suburban Terminus.
21	**521/621** (Finchley Depot)	North Finchley Terminus and Holborn/ Farringdon Street Loop via Finsbury Park	
9	**609** (Holloway Depot)	Barnet and Moorgate, Finsbury Square via Highgate	

2. New Trolleybus Route.

651—Normal hours—St. Gabriels Road, Cricklewood and Barnet.
Peak hours—Golders Green Station and Barnet.

3. Tram Routes to be Withdrawn.

13—Highgate and Aldersgate.
19—Barnet and Tottenham Court Road.
51—Wood Green Station (Piccadilly Line) and Aldersgate.

4. Alterations to existing Tram Routes.

Route 71—Aldersgate and Aldgate will be curtailed to operate between Wood Green Station (Piccadilly Line) and Aldgate via Bruce Grove.

Route 39a will be renumbered 39 and will operate only between Wood Green Station (Piccadilly Line) and Bruce Grove Station.

Route 41—Winchmore Hill and Moorgate will operate partly from Wood Green and partly from Holloway Depots.

FINCHLEY

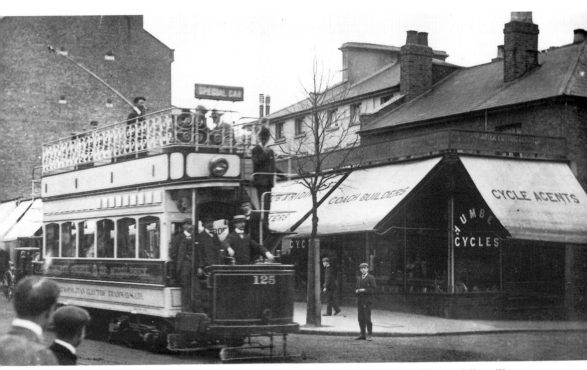

19. Car 125 is pictured in High Street, North Finchley on 19th May 1905. This was the first trial trip over the new lines and served to instruct the MET staff who are grouped round the motorman. The watching public will get their turn on 7th June at the official opening. (D.Jones Coll.)

20. Car 111 again, this time depicted at Tally Ho Corner as it approaches the junction with Ballards Lane. Note the splendid tram standard cum street light on the left of the picture. (B.J.Cross Coll.)

Tally-Ho Corner, Finchley. No. 1933.

21. Crowds gather for the start of the 1912 Finchley Carnival. The driver of car 125 seems to be preparing to set off as soon as possible before he gets tangled up with all the festivities. In the distance can be glimpsed an MET top covered car. (B.J.Cross Coll.)

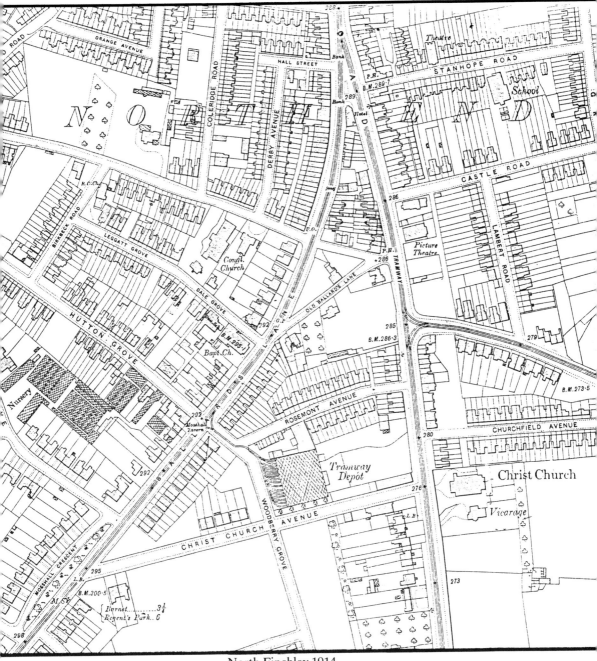

North Finchley 1914

22. The vehicle shown here had a colourful history. Reputedly it was one of the trams converted to carry a searchlight in the First World War. In the late 1920s it was again in the limelight when it collided with a bus at Ponders End causing four fatalities amongst the bus passengers. After the Ministry of Transport inquiry and subsequent court case, car 118 was scrapped. (B.J.Cross Coll.)

23. On 1st February 1931 the first batch of a new type of tram, the Feltham, began to appear on the streets of Finchley. These luxurious vehicles transformed tram travel - one newspaper likened them to "ocean liners" as opposed to the "paddle steamer" image of the older, mainly wooden vehicles they were replacing. Here car 339 waits to transport us in comfort all the way to Holborn. (J.B.Gent Coll.)

24. The Felthams obviously took the eye of the postcard publishers, who wished to present Finchley in the most up-to-date light. Car 326 waits outside the Tally Ho as work proceeds on reconstructing Woolworths opposite. (J.B.Gent Coll.)

25. We look north from the Tally Ho on a scene filled with three tramcars and sundry other motorised vehicles. Inspite of the increased traffic there are still plenty of parking spaces. In the centre of the picture stand a number of tramway officials amongst intending passengers. A notice promotes return fares to Barnet and Highgate of fourpence and sixpence respectively. (B.J.Cross Coll.)

26. Although a new gyratory traffic system incorporating a tram station was promoted by the MET, it was left to London Transport to finish the job in 1934/35. A Feltham on route 45 turns from Kingsway into Ballards Lane. In the background another Feltham enters Woodhouse Road. An older ex-MET car is seen on the extreme left of the picture, it is working route 60 to Paddington. (J.B.Gent Coll.)

27. Claudette Colbert and Charles Boyer are starring in the latest film release, whilst OXO offers some health advice which would not stand up to the scrutiny of today's advertising standards people! Meanwhile on the tramway front, car 878 is about to complete its journey with the front indicator already turned to MOORGATE. The motorman will shortly guide his charge round the corner into Ballards Lane and then right again into Nether Street tram station. (D.W.K.Jones)

21 NTH. FINCHLEY — WOOD GRN. — HOLBORN
Via Friern Barnet Road, Bounds Green Road, Wood
Green, Green Lanes, Manor House, Seven Sisters Road,
Finsbury Park, Holloway, Caledonian Road, Barnsbury,
Kings Cross, Grays Inn Road.
Service Interval 4—5 mins.   Journey time 60 mins.
Through fare, 9d.

	MON. to FRI.		SATURDAY		SUNDAY	
	First	Last	First	Last	First	Last
Tally Ho Corner to Holborn..............	5 50	5 58 10 31	5 58	6 7 10 30	7 54	10 35
Tally Ho Corner to Finsbury Park.......	5 25	16 11 40	5 25	16 12 25	7 54	12 29
Tally Ho Corner to Wood Green.........	5 25	16 12 50	5 25	16 12 50	7 14	12 50
Wood Green to Finsbury Park...........	3 14	4 7 11 59	3 14	4 7 12 44	7 14	12 49
		4 35		4 35		
Wood Green to Holborn.................	3 14	4 7 10 50	3 14	4 7 10 49	7 14	10 55
		6 12		6 13		
Holborn to Tally Ho Corner............	4 0	4 48 11 30	4 0	4 48 11 30	7 54	11 33
		6 53		6 53		
Holborn to Wood Green................	4 0	4 48 11 30	4 0	4 48 11 30	7 54	11 33
		6 53		6 53		
Wood Green to Tally Ho Corner........	4 37	5 4 12 29	4 37	5 4 12 30	8 30	12 30

North Finchley 1936

28. On the right of the picture car 2113 is about to set course for Finchley Depot. Sister car 2074 waits to clear the points and go left. By the time of this photo tram routes 60 and 45 had already been replaced by trolleybuses; this conversion took place on 2nd August 1936. (J.A.Pullen)

29. That cultural icon of the 1930s, the de-luxe Gaumont cinema, looms behind car 614. Increasingly the trams were seen as old fashioned in the face of greater private car traffic and the inevitable desire of the London Transport planners to "move with the times". (R.J.Harley Coll.)

30. The lad in the school cap hangs on tightly before the Feltham on service 21 swings round the corner. The tram behind is another former MET vehicle, now painted in LT livery, it will proceed along the Great North Road to Whetstone and High Barnet. (A.D.Packer Coll.)

550.—ROAD RECONSTRUCTION—TALLY HO CORNER—SERVICES Nos. 45 AND 60.

Notice to Inspectors, Motormen and Conductors.

As from the first car on Sunday, 20th January, 1935, the following arrangements will apply :—

Cars on Services Nos. 45 and 60 will turn at the crossover opposite Friern Park and proceed to Pole No. 169 up track, Great North Road, to pick up passengers. They will then proceed via Great North Road and the new road into Ballards Lane for the up journey and stop at Pole No. 10 (Woodberry Grove).

31. We move in closer to the junction of Kingsway and Woodhouse Road. The two Felthams have just traversed the latter thorough-fare and they provide evidence of the intensive service offered on route 21.
(R.J.Harley Coll.)

This traffic circular was issued by London Transport in September 1935. It is to be hoped that the present operating staff at the National Tramway Museum are not put off by all these official instructions! More details on Car 331 can be found in the Rolling Stock section.

735.—" FELTHAM " CAR 2168—OPERATION OF CENTRE DOORS.

The motorman is responsible for the operation of opening the doors.

The door control button should be operated when approaching a stopping place. This sets the doors to automatically open as car comes to a standstill.

The car cannot again be started until the doors are closed.

Doors can only be closed by the Conductor.

The three door control buttons are located over the doors.

To close doors, operate No. 1 button.

Doors can be opened by conductor by operating buttons 2 and 3 simultaneously.

Emergency handles are also provided over each pair of doors to release the air from the door engines to allow the doors to be opened by hand.

These handles are provided for emergency purposes only and must not be used for ordinary service requirements.

Duties at Terminus.

When changing over at the terminus, the following must be strictly carried out in the order given :—

(1) Place the second trolley on the wire. **Warning**—On no account may both trolleys be off the wire.

(2) The motorman to set the change-over switch while both trolleys are on the wire.

(3) Remove the trolley not required from the wire and place it under the trolley hook.

575.—AUTOMATIC POINTS AT TALLY HO CORNER—SERVICES Nos. 9, 19, 21, 45, 60.

Notice to Staff—Finchley and Holloway Depots.

Automatic points have been installed in the new road between Great North Road and Ballards Lane and in Ballards Lane and must be operated as follows :—

Points in the new road.

Cars turning south must pass under actuating skate with power ON. Cars turning north must pass under skate with power OFF.

Points in Ballards Lane between Poles Nos. 5 and 6.

Cars proceeding north on main road must pass under actuating skate at Pole No. 6 with power ON. Cars proceeding to tramway platform in Nether Street, must pass under skate with power OFF.

The points to the tracks alongside the platform will be operated by the Inspector on duty.

Service No. 19 cars going into service from depot will proceed to and turn at the top crossover Friern Park, as now.

32. Unusually for the 19s this turn is worked by an ex-LCC car rather than the customary ex-MET type H car. On the left stands a solitary dark green trolleybus standard waiting for the overhead crews to erect span wires for the March 1938 conversion. (R.J.Harley Coll.)

33. Electric, horse and internal combustion engine power meet by the triangular junction with Woodhouse Road. Car 118 is again caught on camera, but this time it is heading south towards Highgate. On the extreme left of the picture a member of the permanent way department is cleaning out the point blades. (D.Jones Coll.)

35. We return to the corner of Kingsway and Ballards Lane to witness this former LCC class E/1 car on service 9. Note the conductor who is leaning against the controller on the rear platform whilst filling out his time sheet. (J.A.Pullen)

34. So the story goes, this line up was part of a publicity shot staged in Woodhouse Road. Car 299 certainly has more of a physical presence than the adjacent open top motor bus and the smaller motor cab. An LCC tram is waiting patiently to get past. (D.Jones Coll.)

36. Car 2167 (ex-MET experimental Feltham 330) is seen in North Finchley on London Transport route 45; this service (formerly route 40) was renumbered by LT on 3rd October 1934. This was to avoid confusion with ex-LCC service 40 which ran in Southeast London. (D.W.K.Jones)

LIST OF ROUTES WITH PARTICULARS OF TIMES AND FARES.

Route	ROUTE	Weekdays First Car	Weekdays Last Car	Sundays First Car	Sundays Last Car	FARE
9	NORTH FINCHLEY... & Time 60 mins. Interval 8 mins. W-days 5-6 mins. Sun.	a.m. 5 45	p.m. 11 34	a.m. 8 23	p.m. 11 42	Fare 8d.
	MOORGATE ...	5 27	11 11	7 29	11 7	
18	WOOD GREEN & Time 12 mins. Interval 8 mins. W-days 6 mins. Sun.	a.m. 5 8	p.m. 11 30	a.m. 8 45	p.m. 11 14	Fare 5d.
	BRUCE GROVE ...	5 20	11 44	9 0	11 28	
19	BARNET ... & Time 62 mins. Interval 8 mins. W-days 8 mins. Sun.	a.m. 5 54	p.m. *11 54	a.m. 9 7	p.m. *11 40 10 46	Fare 9d.
	EUSTON ... * To Tally Ho Corner	5 23	10 51	8 47	10 39	
21	NORTH FINCHLEY... (Woodhouse Road) & Time 64 mins. Interval 6 mins. W-days 6 mins. Sun.	a.m. *5 0 6 17	p.m. *12 13 10 6	a.m. 8 53	p.m. *12 13 10 29	Fare 9d.
	HOLBORN ... † To Finsbury Park * From Finsbury Park	*4 22 7 20	11 8	*8 13 8 34	*11 37 11 13	
25 W'days. only.	NEW SOUTHGATE (STATION) & Interval 8 mins.	Mon.-Fri. 6 31	Mon.-Fri. 6 10	Sats. 6 31	Sats. 4 18	Fare 7d.
	EUSTON ... Rush hour service only.	7 23	7 2	7 23	5 10	
26	ENFIELD TOWN & Time 9 mins. Interval 8 mins. W-days 7 mins. Sun.	Weekdays a.m. 5 32	Weekdays midt. 12 0	Sundays. a.m. 10 10	Sundays. p.m. 11 54	Fare 1½d.
	PONDERS END ...	5 23	11 50	10 0	11 44	
27	EDMONTON & Time 51 mins. Interval 3 mins. W-days 3 mins. Sun.	a.m. 6 38	p.m. 8 13	a.m. 9 32	p.m. 11 0	Fare 7d.
	EUSTON ROAD ... Morning and Evening only.	7 31	7 48	10 20	10 36	

Route	ROUTE	Weekdays First Car	Weekdays Last Car	Sundays First Car	Sundays Last Car	FARE
29	ENFIELD TOWN & Time 62 mins. Interval 5 mins. W-days 5 mins. Sun.	a.m. 5 15	p.m. 11 20	a.m. 9 24	p.m. 11 18	Fare 9d.
	EUSTON ROAD ...	5 26	10 54	8 22	10 38	
29 & 31	WINCHMORE HILL... & Time 53 mins. Interval 5 mins. W-days 5 mins. Sun.	a.m. 5 24	p.m. 11 29	a.m. 9 33	p.m. 11 27	Fare 8d.
	EUSTON ROAD ... * To Wood Green	5 26	11 22	8 22	10 56	
30 Evenings only.	ALEXANDRA PALACE & Time 15 mins. Thurs., Sats. & Suns. Interval 12 mins.	p.m. 6 18	p.m. 10 30	p.m. *5 47	p.m. 10 15	Fare 2d.
	THE WELLINGTON ...	6 1	10 13	5 30	10 18	
32 Evenings only.	ALEXANDRA PALACE & Time 9 mins. Thurs., Sats. & Suns. Interval 4 mins.	p.m. 6 11	p.m. 10 35	p.m. 5 41	p.m. 10 35	Fare 1½d.
	WOOD GREEN ...	6 0	10 24	5 30	10 24	
32	WOOD GREEN & Time 4 mins. Interval 12 mins. W-days 8 mins. Sat. & Sun.	a.m. 8 0	p.m. 11 0	a.m. 10 0	p.m. 10 48	Fare 1d.
	WOOD GREEN STN. ...	8 6	11 6	10 6	10 54	
39 W'days. only.	BRUCE GROVE & Time 52 mins. Interval 8 mins.	Mon.-Fri. 6 40	Mon.-Fri. 8 36 *10 15	Sats. 6 40	Sats. 9 43 *11 30	Fare 8d.
	ALDERSGATE ... * To Finsbury Park via Wood Green.	7 31	9 20	7 31	10 37	
42	TOTTERIDGE LANE... & Time 36 mins. Interval 8 mins. W-days 8 mins. Sun.	Weekdays a.m. 6 57	Weekdays p.m. 9 0	Sundays a.m. 11 35	Sundays p.m. 11 3	Fare 6d.
	CRICKLEWOOD ...	6 20	8 19	10 56	10 24	
40 42 & 46	NORTH FINCHLEY... & Time 19 mins. Interval 2 mins. W-days 4 mins. Sun.	a.m. 5 0	p.m. 11 45	a.m. 9 0	p.m. 11 10	Fare 4d.
	GOLDERS GREEN ...	5 41	12 25	9 39	11 52	

MET services as listed in the 1922 map.

37. We now arrive at North Finchley tram station, situated behind the Gaumont in Nether Street. The vehicle on view, car 2481, is now showing its age, having first emerged in 1904 as type B car 26. Later in 1912-16 Hendon Works fitted it with a top cover. It was withdrawn from service in 1936.
(D.W.K.Jones)

Route	ROUTE	Weekdays		Sundays		FARE
		First Car	Last Car	First Car	Last Car	
40 & 42	NORTH FINCHLEY... ♦ Time 29 mins. Interval 4 mins. W-days 4 mins. Sun. CRICKLEWOOD ...	a.m. 5 0 5 32	p.m. 11 45 12 15	a.m. 9 0 9 30	p.m. 11 10 11 42	Fare 5d.
49	EDMONTON ... ♦ Time 47 mins. Interval 4 mins. W-days 4 mins. Sun. LIVERPOOL ST. STN.	a.m. 4 57 5 48	p.m. 11 14 12 3	a.m. 7 45 7 17	p.m. 11 16 11 37	Fare 6d.
49	WALTHAM CROSS ... ♦ Time 73 mins. Interval 6 mins. Sats. 8 mins. Sun. LIVERPOOL ST. STN. * To Stamford Hill.	a.m. 6 37 5 48	p.m. 10 58 10 33	p.m. 2 30 1 17	p.m. *11 34 10 46 (Sats. only) 10 21	Fare 11d.
				During rush hours Mon. to Fri.		
51	MUSWELL HILL ... ♦ Time 56 mins. Interval 8 mins. W-days 8 mins. Sun. BLOOMSBURY ... * From Wood Green † To Wood Green	a.m. *3 57 6 15 †4 41 5 33	p.m. 11 19 †12 9 11 7	a.m. 10 5 †11 16 10 52	p.m. *11 40 10 13 †11 0 10 52	Fare 6d.
54	HENDON (Colindale) ... ♦ Time 23 mins. Interval 6 mins. W-days 6 mins. Sun. WILLESDEN GN. STN.	a.m. 4 50 5 16	p.m. 11 36 12 0	a.m. 8 41 9 5	p.m. 11 20 11 45	Fare 4d.
56	CANON'S PARK ... ♦ Time 37 mins. Interval 12 mins. W-days WILLESDEN GN. STN.	a.m. 8 0 7 16	p.m. 10 42 9 58	a.m. 9 29 9 5	p.m. 10 32 9 56	Fare 6d.
59	EDMONTON (Tn. Hall) ... ♦ Time 55 mins. Interval 6 mins. W-days 8 mins. Sun. HOLBORN ... † To Finsbury Park	a.m. 4 25 5 23	p.m. †11 59 11 37 1 0	a.m. 8 37 9 30	p.m. 11 9 mdt. 12 0	Fare 8d.

Route	ROUTE	Weekdays		Sundays		FARE
		First Car	Last Car	First Car	Last Car	
60	CRICKLEWOOD ... ♦ Time 42 mins. Interval 6 mins. W-days 8 mins. Sun. PADDINGTON ... * To Jubilee Clock.	a.m. 5 27 5 5	p.m. *12 15 12 0 11 27	a.m. 8 58 9 7	p.m. *11 47 11 10 11 4	Fare 7d.
62	SUDBURY ... ♦ Time 46 mins. Interval 6 mins. W-days 8 mins. Sun. PADDINGTON ... * From Stonebridge Park. † To Stonebridge Park.	a.m. *4 9 5 50 *4 43 4 55	p.m. 11 42 *12 43 11 2 11 12	a.m. *8 28 9 0 †9 0	p.m. 11 10 *12 0 10 36 11 12	Fare 8d.
		Wmbly		Wmbly		
64	ACTON ... ♦ Rush Hours Only. Time 35 mins. Interval 6 mins. PADDINGTON ...	Mon.-Fri. Morning. a.m. 7 0 5 30 Evening. p.m. 6 46 4 28	a.m. 8 36 6 18 p.m. 7 52 5 34	Sats. Morning. a.m. 7 0 11 21 Afternoon. p.m. 6 46 12 2	a.m. 8 36 1 15 Afternoon. p.m. 7 52 1 56	Fare 6d.
66	ACTON ... ♦ Time 34 mins. *Interval 6 mins. W-days 12 mins. Sun. CRICKLEWOOD ... *Additional cars between Acton and Jubilee Clock. †To Harlesden	a.m. 5 25 5 20	p.m. *11 57 11 18	a.m. 9 0 9 5	p.m. 10 45 10 55	Fare 6d.
19 & 69	NORTH FINCHLEY... ♦ Time 46 mins. Interval 4 mins. W-days EUSTON ROAD ...	a.m. 4 37 5 22	p.m. 11 49 12 36	a.m. 8 4 8 47	p.m. 11 3 11 48	Fare 7d.
79	WALTHAM CROSS ... ♦ Time 79 mins. Interval 6 mins. W-days 8 mins. Sun. SMITHFIELD MKT. ... † To Finsbury Park (1) To Edmonton.	a.m. 4 51 5 50	p.m. 11 35 10 14 (1) 11 37 10 39	a.m. 9 5 9 40	p.m. †11 15 10 16 11 35 10 52	Fare 1/1

38. A trio of contrasting tram styles is seen on parade in the tram station; leading the pack is former London United type W car 199, now masquerading as LT car 2404. Behind is Feltham car 2090 which was former MET car 346. This vehicle later saw service in South London and was sold to Leeds City Transport in 1951. Bringing up the rear of the group is a standard E/1 class car. (R.J.Harley Coll.)

606.—TALLY HO CORNER TERMINUS.

Notice to Motormen and Conductors—Finchley and Stonebridge Depots.

Cars entering the terminus on either track must stop short of the single track so as to enable another car to pass if necessary.

39. It looks like car 2280 (ex-MET type G car 235) is going to depart first on the long haul through West London to terminate at Paddington. The motorman of car 882 takes his time before heading south to the City terminus by Ropemaker Street near Moorgate. This area is featured in *Holborn and Finsbury Tramways*. (D.Jones Coll.)

607.—TALLY HO CORNER OPERATION.

Notice to Motormen and Conductors—Finchley Depot.

On and from Sunday, 3rd March, all reliefs for Service No. 19 cars will take place as follows :—

On " Up " journey : at Pole No. 160, Gt. North Road, opposite Rosemont Avenue.

On " Down " journey : at Pole No. 4, Ballards Lane.

All cars running into depot from direction of Golders Green, Highgate or Wood Green must proceed via the Terminus platform.

40. A classic study looking east along Nether Street reveals Feltham 2118 (ex-MET type UCC car 374) and an unidentified E/1 class car. It must be remembered that the LCC referred to their vehicles by *classes*, whilst the MET, LUT and SMET company tramways divided their fleets into *types*. (G.N.Southerden)

41. Car 2407 is another refugee from West London, having started its life as LUT type W car 161. In 1928 it was fitted with a top cover similar to those fitted to type T tramcars; it was then reclassified, quite logically, type WT. After having admired this tram, there might just be time to a catch a Harold Lloyd comedy at the cinema opposite. Perhaps the programme would include several of the comedian's death defying stunts dodging Pacific Electric streetcars in Los Angeles! (D.Jones Coll.)

42. The tramway era in North Finchley draws to a close as sunlight strikes car 1074. In the shadows a few passengers stand near the new shelter, whilst opposite, a bus on route 125 and two trolleybuses on route 660 hug the pavement next to the Gaumont. Soon the familiar sound of steel wheels on steel rails will give way to the almost eerie hush of yet more electric trolleybuses. (D.W.K.Jones)

43. In July 1933 before the tram station was open, we discover car 30 about to reverse at the corner of Hall Street. (G.N.Southerden)

44. The next tram we encounter is car 3, an MET type B/2 vehicle which would shortly be renumbered 2467 by LT. It was withdrawn from service in October 1935. (G.N.Southerden)

897.—WORKMAN TRANSFERS VIA TALLY HO AND REVISED TICKETS.

Notice to Inspectors and Conductors—Finchley, Stonebridge, Hendon and Holloway Depots.

Commencing on Monday, 20th January, 1936, the following workman return transfers, change at Tally Ho Corner, will be re-instituted :—

Swan and Pyramids and					Totteridge Lane and				
Mountfield Road	...	...	...	2d.	Church End Station	...	...	...	2d.
Temple Fortune Lane	...	...	...	3d.	Addison Way	...	...	...	3d.
Castle, Child's Hill	...	...	...	4d.	Golders Green Station	...	...	...	4d.
Cricklewood Broadway	...	...	...	5d.	Cricklewood Tavern	...	...	...	5d.

On the same date revised workman tickets with the direct journey sections arranged as far as possible in the same order as those on the ordinary single tickets will be put into operation at Finchley and Stonebridge Depots. At Finchley Depot separate sets of tickets will be used on the vestibule and non-vestibule duties, and in addition new ordinary single tickets will be used on the vestibule duty as soon after 20th January as possible.

45. We look past Ballards Lane Post Office towards Tally Ho Corner. At this time only the northbound track remained wired, this was due to the opening of the tram station and new one way traffic scheme which had removed southbound tramcars from this part of the street. (D.Jones Coll.)

46. Car 2092 (ex-MET car 348, and after 1951, Leeds car 533) has been newly repainted in LT red livery, whilst a sister vehicle in the background still retains its predominantly MET derived white and red livery. Again one can note the almost complete lack of competing motor traffic in this mid 1930s scene. (H.Nicol)

47. Opposite Hutton Grove car 05 stops whilst the motorman places the trolley on the positive wire of the new trolleybus overhead. This strange looking vehicle dating from 1911 was employed to carry sand from Wood Green Depot to other depots on the MET system. It was fitted with windscreens in 1926, and survived until 1938. Latterly its tasks took it into LCC territory with visits to Hampstead Depot and Poplar Wharf adjacent to the nearby car shed. (D.W.K.Jones)

48. Church End, Finchley lies to the west of the town and was first reached by trams in December 1909. This early view shows car 235 in its original state (its final condition is shown in picture 39). The other traffic, such as it was, also favours the well paved area surrounding the tram tracks. (B.J.Cross Coll.)

49. By the corner of Nether Street outside the Railway Hotel we note a tram stop with the fare stage number 14. Aside from car 236 heading off into the distance, the only other event of importance seems to be something going on amongst all the ladies to the right of the picture. (B.J.Cross Coll.)

50. Fare stage 13 was located on Regents Park Road by East End Road. One wonders whether the owner of the horse and cart stationed outside the Queens Head will shortly emerge after his liquid refreshment. Another topic of speculation is whether car 224 can give the upstart motorist a run for his money. (D.Jones Coll.)

FINCHLEY DEPOT

51. Finchley Depot opened in June 1905 on a site at the corner of Woodberry Grove and Rosemont Avenue. The capacity was 60 tramcars which were stabled on 15 tracks. In this picture the nearest tram is on road number 3; by the look of the pile of building materials by roads 10 and 11 conversion work for trolleybuses has already started. (R.J.Harley Coll.)

1154.—WITHDRAWAL OF TRAM SERVICE No. 60.

Notice to Inspectors and Conductors—Wandsworth, Hammersmith and Clapham Depots.

On Sunday, 2nd August, Tram Route No. 60 (Paddington and Finchley) will be withdrawn owing to the commencement of trolleybus operation between Cricklewood and North Finchley. To compensate for the withdrawal of the trams, workman transfers will be issued for journeys to and from points between Paddington and Jubilee Clock and points between Cricklewood and North Finchley.

Passengers boarding Route No. 28 trams will be issued workman transfer tickets as follows :—

Fare.	Journey.	Change Point.
4d. Workman	Castle, Child's Hill and Scrubs Lane	Jubilee Clock or Craven Park
5d. Workman	Temple Fortune Lane and Scrubs Lane	

Route Nos. 660-664-666 4d. and 5d. workman tickets will be put into the 28 boxes for this purpose and passengers desiring to travel to points beyond Temple Fortune Lane must be advised to book again on the second car from the point of expiry of the transfer ticket.
Specimens of these tickets will be exhibited in the depots.

52. We peer into the depot yard on possibly the last evening of tramway operation. A blaze of lights illuminates a tramcar rostered on service 19 to Tottenham Court Road, meanwhile several rows of trolleybuses await their call to duty. (A.J.Watkins Coll.)

53. The same spot as the previous photo, but now we witness a Feltham as it noses out of the depot yard to take up service on the 21s. On the left sits a tower wagon drafted in to erect the new overhead. (J.A.Pullen)

54. Before any thoughts of tramway replacement became current, car 164 occupies the lead track to road 7 of the depot. The date is 4th August 1929. In those days the enthusiastic amateur was generally welcomed on to tramway premises; this is in marked contrast to the "keep out" mentality which greets today's transport fans. We must grateful to the MET officials who allowed Geoffrey Southerden to take this view. (G.N.Southerden)

55. Remember when public transport vehicles were regularly cleaned! Two depot staff demonstrate how to keep the fleet spick and span. (D.Jones Coll.)

56. Another view taken on 4th August 1929, this time through the lens of Dr.Hugh Nicol, one of this country's most admired tramway photographers. Cars 107, 84 and 75 belong to type A, and the latter has a non-standard brass top controller. On the extreme right is type H car 302. (H.Nicol)

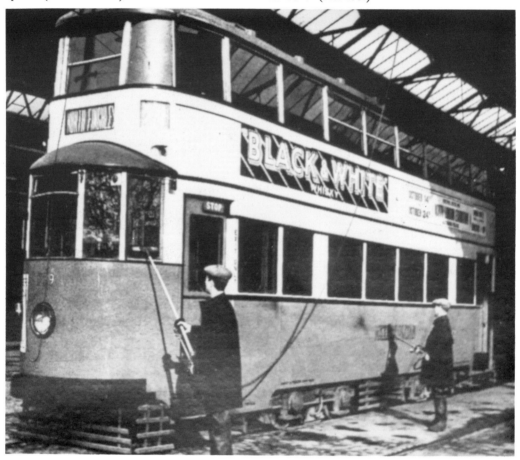

57. During 1930 Finchley Depot was redesigned to to be able to take the longer Feltham type cars, one of which is seen in this picture. Out of camera shot in front of these trams is a newly installed traverser which shifted cars sideways to the appropriate stabling road. (R.J.Harley Coll.)

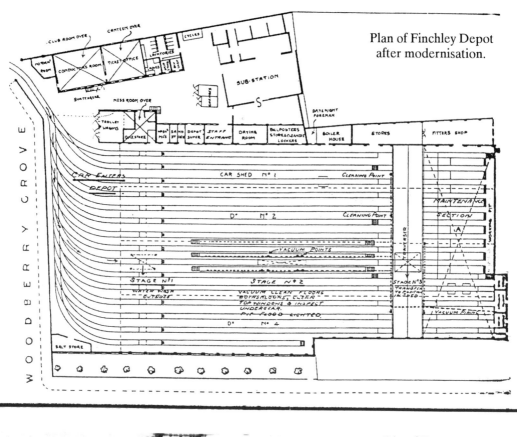

Plan of Finchley Depot after modernisation.

GOLDERS GREEN

59. The impetus for growth in Golders Green was given by the arrival of the "Hampstead Tube" in 1907. Two years later the MET came on the scene and a lively interchange of passengers between the two electrified forms of transport ensued. Here passengers transfer to the Underground which was extended to Brent and Hendon in November 1923. The final extension of what was to become the Northern Line occurred in 1924 when Edgware was reached. (D.Jones Coll.)

58. The scene looks wet and univiting as a lone tram ekes out its last days before being sent to the scrapyard. The replacement trolleybuses were also cleared out in January 1962 and the area, by now renamed Finchley Garage, became a haven of diesel fumes. Such was its melancholy fate. (C.F.Klapper)

60. A fine picture of car 4 as the conductor checks for any stragglers before he rings the bell for departure. As befits a photo taken during the US prohibition era - thankfully not enforced in the UK - the adverts on the side of the car maintain a neat balance between alcohol and temperance! (H.Nicol)

61. The sleek, modern lines of experimental car 320 stand comparison with present day designs. No wonder passengers would let older cars go past so that they could board the new super-tram. Here the car pauses a few seconds at Golders Green before gliding away to North Finchley. (G.N.Southerden)

62. A landscape view of Golders Green reveals the railway bridge carrying the tube north to Edgware. In the foreground a General motor bus begins its journey to West Norwood, deep in South London. Tramway enthusiasts could also reach West Norwood, but by a more circuitous route than that taken by the route 2 bus. (B.J.Cross Coll.)

63. The next experimental tram to grace Golders Green by its presence is car 330. Already the station area had become an important North London transport centre. Underground trains, trams and central buses all swapped passengers, and in 1929 Golders Green became the first London terminus for Green Line coaches. (G.N.Southerden)

Golders Green 1936

64. Many tales are told about the number of people who could cram into a tramcar, especially when said tramcar was not under official scrutiny from an inspector or member of the local constabulary. Car 75 here demonstrates its crowd swallowing abilities at Golders Green on Whit Monday 1919. Most of these folk were no doubt intent on a day out exploring the countryside north of Barnet. Such excursions were promoted by the MET in a series of country walks handbooks. (B.J.Cross Coll.)

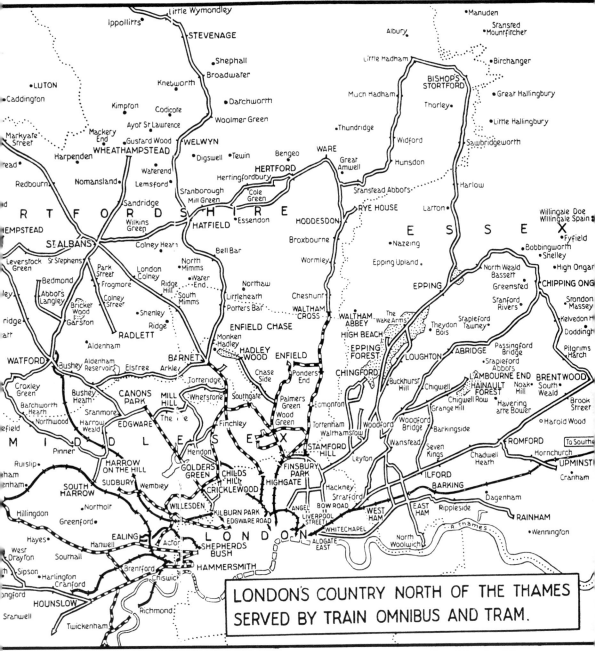

LONDON'S COUNTRY NORTH OF THE THAMES SERVED BY TRAIN OMNIBUS AND TRAM.

Extract from 1922 handbook *London's Country*. This was published to encourage people to explore the countryside, using vari- ous forms of transport offered by the "Combine". Note that the LCC and other municipal tramways do not feature on this map.

65. Several times the MET had proposed a tramway siding with attendant loading islands, but somehow this facility never got built. Ironically in trolleybus days a turning circle was constructed in the station forecourt. In this picture the recently erected war memorial takes centre stage with electric trams to the left and petrol buses to the right. Cars 10 and 14 are from the same batch (type B), but the former was reclassified type B/2 when it received an open balcony top cover. (D.Jones Coll.)

66. Solid Edwardian architecture abounds in Finchley Road as car 12 rumbles sedately past the rather exotic edifice which houses the local cinema. (J.B.Gent Coll.)

EAST FINCHLEY

67. Type C car 164 pauses at the Squires Lane Post Office Stop on Finchley High Road. In the shop window is a small notice marked EMIGRANTS. Doubtless the charms of life in the dominions and colonies attracted some local inhabitants. The tramway company also made its contribution to this exodus by selling four trams to Auckland, New Zealand in 1907. (B.J.Cross Coll.)

68. Outside the bakers in High Road, East Finchley, car 115 halts to set down passengers. This tram still possesses a Wilson Bennett wire mesh lifeguard which was later replaced by the standard Hudson and Bowring wooden slatted type. The centre poles supporting the overhead were removed in 1913-14 as they had the unfortunate knack of inducing more and more motorists to collide with them! (D.Jones Coll.)

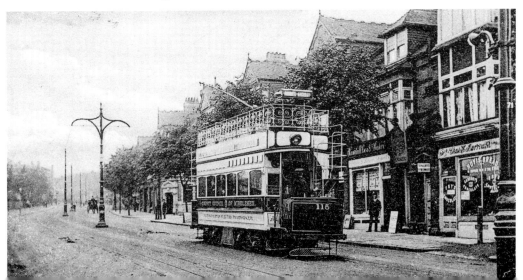

69. Not long before the end of the trams in Finchley, new trolleybus traction poles are replacing their older tramway counterparts. Note the widely spaced double tracks and the two overtaking motorists eager to make progress up the Great North Road.
(H.B.Priestley)

HIGHGATE ARCHWAY

70. Archway Road, Highgate is the setting for car 114 as it passes the police station by Bishops Road. (D.Jones Coll.)

71. The conductor of car 128 shows a courtesy common in the first decade of the twentieth century as he helps ladies and children to descend safely from the car. As the destination of the tram is HIGHGATE ARCHWAY, this dates the view to between June and December 1905 when the service was extended to Archway Tavern. (D.Jones Coll.)

72. The faster electric trams had a distinct edge over horse drawn traffic especially on gradients like the one shown here. In the distance is Highgate Archway which carries Hornsey Lane over Archway Road. (J.B.Gent Coll.)

73. This postcard was marketed under the title *Trams - Archway Road*. The new marvels of electric traction were certainly something to write home about. Car 129 of type A was later renumbered 2465 by London Transport and finally met its Waterloo in December 1935. (B.J.Cross Coll.)

74. An assorted group of tradespeople and an accordian player gather in Archway Road as car 104 is about to move off. Just above the tram can be discerned the thicker wires of the power feed to the overhead. These wires delivered 550 volts DC to the copper trolley wire suspended about 21ft./6.4 metres above the highway. Section power feeds occurred at half mile/750 metre intervals. (J.B.Gent Coll.)

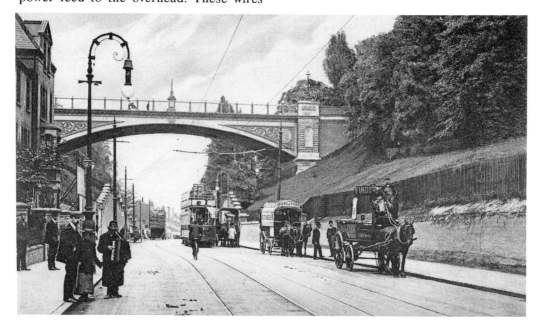

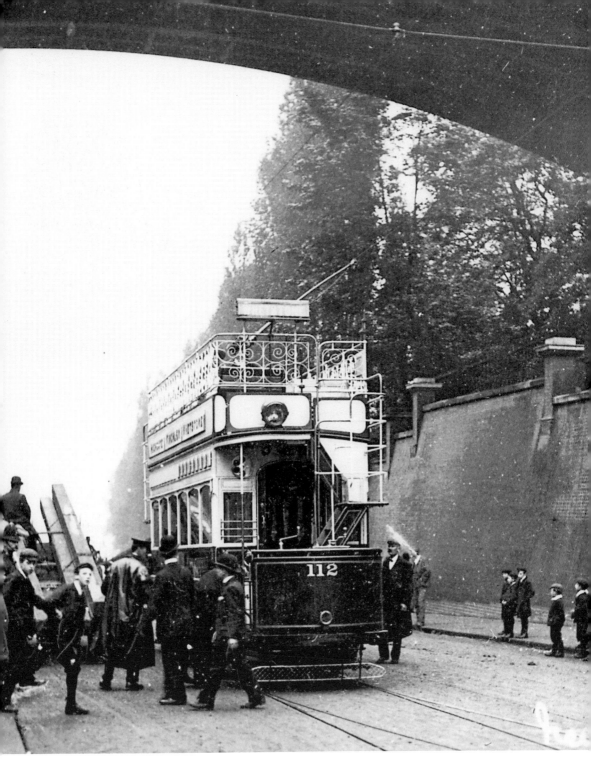

75. A crowd of interested spectators and the obligatory policeman turn out for one of the first trial runs on the Archway to Totteridge Lane, Whetstone route. The official inspection was on 19th May 1905 and revenue service commenced on 7th June. One could do the whole journey for the princely sum of 3d (just over 1p)! (D.Jones Coll.)

76. Car 120 is in brand new condition as it passes under Highgate Archway. The former county boundary between London and Middlesex crosses the road at this point. (B.J.Cross Coll.)

77. LCC car 878 regains its home territory as it enters the county of London. On the other side of the road a single decker motor bus lumbers up the hill on its journey to Colney Hatch Lane. In 1973 long after the trams had disappeared, this section of Archway Road was rebuilt as a dual carriageway. (J.B.Gent Coll.)

78. The area was the centre of high drama on 23rd June 1906 when the motorman of car 115 lost control of his tram on the gradient south of Archway. The vehicle then gathered speed and after colliding with several other road users, it struck another MET tram waiting at the terminus. This view shows some of the mayhem after the casualties had been taken to hospital. Tragically three people lost their lives in the accident. (B.J.Cross Coll.)

79. We now look past the Archway Tavern along Archway Road where an MET open top car 208 is loading passengers. In front of the tram is a change pit where cars altered current collection from overhead to conduit. Several permanent way workers are engaged on maintaining the road surface adjacent to the rails. (B.J.Cross Coll.)

80. The date is March 1938 and a former MET tram, now in LT colours, receives the plough for operation over the conduit system. The intricacies of this method are described in *Southwark and Deptford Tramways*. (R.J.Harley Coll.)

81. Car 2201 (ex-MET type H car 269) is pictured at the change pit outside the Archway Tavern. This vehicle also appears on picture 9. Note the crew members and change pit attendants standing next to the plough forks which are scattered in the middle of the carriageway. In a few days the 43 bus will be joined by trolleybus route 609 and the southern section of tram service 19 will be replaced by a strengthened bus route 134 between Archway and Euston Road. (R.J.Harley Coll.)

82. In happier days we observe car 199 which has been maintained in splendid condition. On the dash is a warning triangle for motorists who were following the tram too closely. This tram is working route 69 to North Finchley which was withdrawn in October 1931. This rush hour service was normally operated by LCC cars. (H.Nicol)

83. One o'clock on a sunny afternoon and to the left of the picture an LCC car prepares to leave on service 13. In the distance an MET top covered car coasts down the hill towards the change pit. (J.B.Gent Coll.)

84. LCC car 1106 stands on the terminal track before through services were inaugurated. Conduit tramways built by the LCC were opened to Archway on 28th November 1907. A connection was made to the MET tracks on 30th November 1909, but the change pit was not operational until March 1914. (D.Jones Coll.)

85. Car 593 waits at the foot of Highgate Hill as a double deck M class car passes on service 11. The tramways at this location receive further coverage in *Hampstead and Highgate Tramways*. Suffice it to mention here, that the LCC electrified lines up Highgate Hill opened on 25th March 1910. (H.Nicol)

86. In contrast to the previous view we are now presented with a double deck tram on service 35. This was one of the famous Kingsway Subway routes that connected North London with the other half of the capital south of the river. Here ex-Leyton E/3 class car 184 represents the only tram route left in Highgate after the pre-war trolleybus conversion scheme. (R.J.Harley Coll.)

87. The 35 tram soldiered on until 5th April 1952 when it disappeared in favour of the diesel bus. In this picture car 186 makes light work of the snow and ice which was troubling other road users on 29th March 1952. Trams were famous for getting through come what may - fog and winter weather rarely affected their ability to supply reliable public transport. (J.C.Gillham)

ROLLING STOCK

This section deals with MET type C cars and also covers the experimental trams which acted as "test rigs" before the introduction of the famous UCC type "Feltham" vehicles in the early 1930s. Readers are reminded that types B, G and H are described in *Stamford Hill Tramways*.

Type C cars 151-165. Type C/1 cars 192-211. Cars 151-165 were built by Brush at Loughborough in 1906. They seated 32 people inside and 42 on the open top deck. The trucks were to a Brush BB maximum traction design. All 15 members of this type were sent to Hendon Works in 1912-16 for conversion to type C/2. This involved the addition of open balcony top covers and the re-equipping of each car with higher powered motors. In 1926/7 vehicles of this type were again remotored. They were renumbered 2483-2497 by London Transport and were scrapped in 1936.

Cars 192-211 dated from 1908 and were basically similar to type C vehicles, but they were mounted on Mountain and Gibson type 3L maximum traction trucks. These were to become the standard for the MET and they were basically similar to the tried and tested design used under the vast E/1 class of the LCC. Plough carriers were also fitted to enable these trams to work joint services into the County of London. All 20 trams of this type were rebuilt with fully enclosed top covers in 1929. The lower saloon of each tram also received transverse seating which altered the capacity to 28 inside and 46 on the top deck. London Transport renumbered the series 2282-2301 in 1933, and the end came in 1938.

88. Features to note on car 203 include: the headlamp positioned in the top canopy, the intricate wrought iron work round the top deck, the EIGHT WHEEL BRAKES warning triangle, the truck mounted plough carrier and the Metropolitan Stage Carriage No. 9716. This vehicle was top covered in 1929 and became LT car 2293. It was scrapped in March 1938. (H.Nicol)

89. This is the lower saloon of car 193. The standard of craftsmanship is to be admired and the predominantly wooden interior positively gleams with different types of timber used for the ceiling and bulkhead doors. Seating consisted of longitudinal benches, and if the car were full and the seats occupied, then leather straps provide a convenient handhold for those travellers obliged to stand. Note the advertisements on and above the windows; a strict no smoking rule was enforced in the lower saloon. (MET)

90. Life on the top deck of an MET car was for the more robust, hardy types who could smoke and enjoy the sunshine - and suffer being drenched in the rain and frozen to the seat in severe winters! The trolley standard is in the centre of this view and the upper deck guard rails are constructed to a height of 3ft. 6ins./1067mm above the deck floor. The extra guard rails at the end of the car are to safeguard passengers in case of a trolley spring failing and bringing the pole down. (B.J.Cross Coll.)

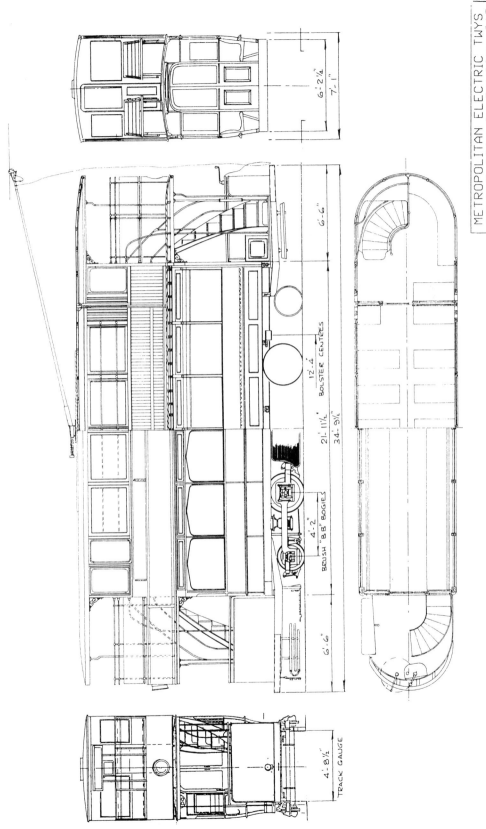

METROPOLITAN ELECTRIC TWYS
DOUBLE DECK 8W BALCONY CAR

BUILT BRUSH 1906 REBUILT 1912/16 | SCALE 4 MM = 1 FOOT
TYPE C/2   FLEET No 151-165

DRAWING No TC586

6'-2½"
7'-1"

6'-6"

12'-4"
BOLSTER CENTRES

21'-11½"
34'-9½"

4'-2"
BRUSH "BB" BOGIES

6'-6"

4'-8½"
TRACK GAUGE

SCALE
FEET 0 1 2 3 4 5 6 7 8 9 10 11 12

DRAWN BY:-TERRY RUSSELL, "CHACESIDE", ST.LEONARDS PARK, HORSHAM, W.SUSSEX. RH13 6EG.
SEND 3 FIRST CLASS STAMPS FOR COMPLETE LIST OF PUBLIC TRANSPORT DRAWINGS.

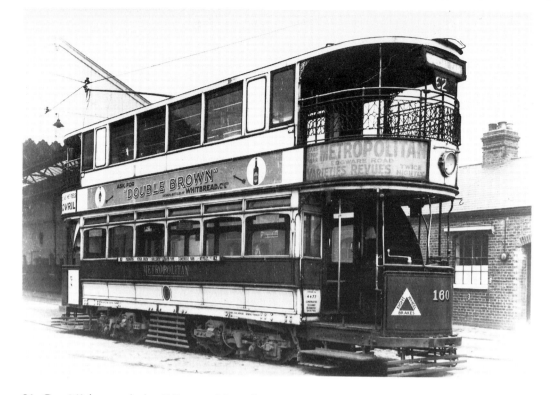

91. Car 160 is seen in its C/2 state. Note the Brush BB maximum traction trucks which are "reversed" i.e. the smaller "pony" wheels are leading. The more normal London arrangement was to place these pony wheels behind the larger driving wheels. Note also the six bar "dog gate" between the trucks; this allegedly prevented inquisitive canines from getting stuck under the car. (D.Jones Coll.)

92. The final incarnation of MET car 193 is seen here disguised as LT car 2483. Differences compared to the previous picture, aside from the LT red and cream livery, are mainly centred on the top deck balconies which have lost their attractive special work in favour of rather bland looking metal sheets. (G.N.Southerden)

Experimental Tramcars.

MET car 318 "Bluebell".

In the mid 1920s the MET manager, C.J. Spencer, turned his attention to improving the fleet. Sensibly he suggested pooling resources with the rolling stock engineers of the London General Omnibus Company which was in the same financial group as the three London company tramways - MET, LUT and SMET. Advice was also sought from the underground railway side of the conglomerate, especially with regard to equipping the new cars with air operated doors. Car 318 eventually emerged from Hendon Works in 1927; it was painted in a pleasant shade of pale blue with white window frames. The vehicle entered service on 12th March 1927 on route 40 from Barnet to Cricklewood. After the fatal accident of June 1927 the tram was rebuilt and re-emerged from Hendon almost a year later. In its final form it served in the Finchley area under both MET and LT regimes before being sent for scrap in 1936.

93. The mess that was left after the tragic collision on Barnet Hill - note that the panelling and the dash have been pushed by the impact into the lower saloon of the car. Aluminium sheeting was used for most of the body panelling. The original lightweight fender can also be noted. (D.Jones Coll.)

94. This shot of the lower deck of car 318 shows the two-and-one tranverse seats which were upholstered in green moquette. Top deck passengers were accommodated on 18 transverse double seats which were covered in green leatherette. The whole car was some four tons lighter than a comparable MET type H car. (MET)

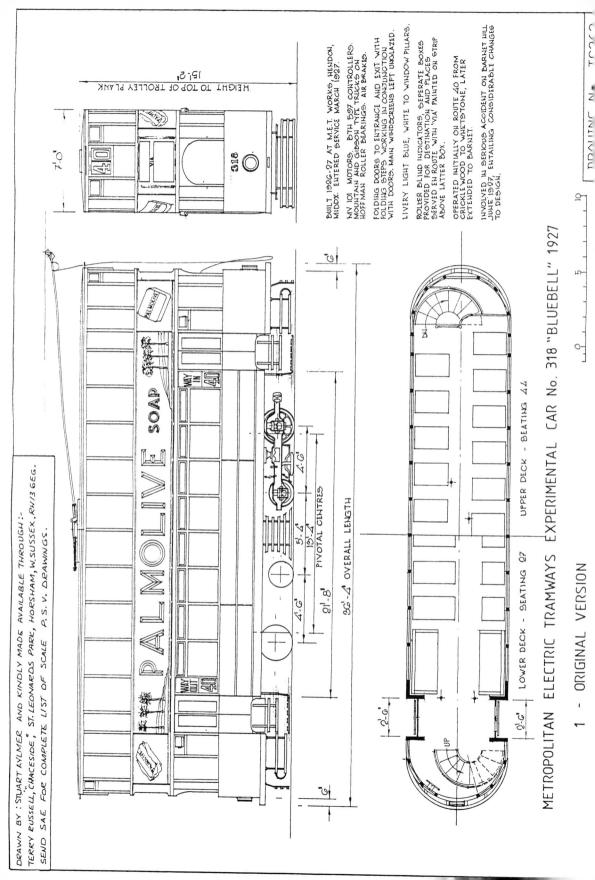

7'-0"

HEIGHT TO TOP OF TROLLEY PLANK

15'-2"

318

BUILT 1926-27 AT M.E.T. WORKS, HENDON,
MIDDX. ENTERED SERVICE MARCH 1927.

MV 101 MOTORS, BTH 597 CONTROLLERS.
MOUNTAIN AND GIBSON TYPE TRUCKS ON
HOFFMAN ROLLER BEARINGS. AIR BRAKES.

FOLDING DOORS TO ENTRANCE AND EXIT WITH
FOLDING STEPS WORKING IN CONJUNCTION
WITH DOORS. MAIN WINDSCREENS LEFT UNGLAZED.

LIVERY LIGHT BLUE, WHITE TO WINDOW PILLARS.

ROLLER BLIND INDICATORS, SEPERATE BOXES
PROVIDED FOR DESTINATION AND PLACES
SERVED EN ROUTE WITH 'VIA' PAINTED ON STRIP
ABOVE LATTER BOX.

OPERATED INITIALLY ON ROUTE 40 FROM
CRICKLEWOOD TO WHETSTONE, LATER
EXTENDED TO BARNET.

INVOLVED IN SERIOUS ACCIDENT ON BARNET HILL
JUNE 1927, ENTAILING CONSIDERABLE CHANGES
TO DESIGN.

DRAWING No. TC262

DRAWN BY : STUART AYLMER AND KINDLY MADE AVAILABLE THROUGH:-
TERRY RUSSELL, CHACESIDE, " ST. LEONARDS PARK, HORSHAM, W.SUSSEX. RH/3 6EG.
SEND SAE FOR COMPLETE LIST OF SCALE P.S.V. DRAWINGS.

PALMOLIVE SOAP

WAY IN 40

40

WAY OUT 40

6"

4'-6"   5'-4"   4'-6"
         15'-4"
      PIVOTAL CENTRES

21'-8"

36'-4" OVERALL LENGTH

6"

DN

UP

2'-6"   2'-6"

LOWER DECK - SEATING 27   UPPER DECK - SEATING 44

METROPOLITAN ELECTRIC TRAMWAYS EXPERIMENTAL CAR No. 318 "BLUEBELL" 1927

1 - ORIGINAL VERSION

0   5   10

95. The original intention of the white flashes on the dash was to warn motorists of the extra braking power of MET vehicles. Car 318 is seen in its rebuilt state, but still in the pale blue livery. In 1931 this vehicle was repainted in the standard company vermilion (bright signal red) and white. (G.N.Southerden)

96. A final view shows the car in London Transport livery bearing the gold fleet number 2255. Inspite of its modernity the decision makers at 55 Broadway were not impressed and this "one off" vehicle was sent to the scrapyard. (G.N.Southerden)

MET car 319 "Poppy".

The design and construction of this experimental vehicle was entrusted to the staff of the LGOC works at Chiswick. In outline it resembled very much two NS type buses welded together, and it included a projecting driver's cab which was later adopted as standard on type UCC Feltham cars. Lightweight metal construction was adopted throughout and a domed roof in aluminium was fitted. The car appeared in "General" bus red, which was a darker shade than the familiar MET vermilion. It joined the rest of the fleet at Finchley Depot in April 1927 and went for trials on the Whetstone - Cricklewood service. It was subsequently moved to Wood Green Depot and on 16th November Poppy was transferred to

97. A fine portrait of Poppy as it stands at the entrance gates to Hanwell Depot on 13th September 1928. The workings of the front doors and automatic step seem to be occasioning some interest amongst the depot staff. A fitter looks out stoically from the motorman's platform, which, unfortunately for the driver, is still without a windscreen. Bus technology has certainly influenced the placing of two headlights above the cab instead of the traditional tramway single lamp on the dash. (H.Nicol)

the LUT to work services in West London. Here it was renumbered 350 in the LUT fleet, and it passed to London Transport as car 2317. It worked tram route 57 from Shepherds Bush to Hounslow until replacement by trolleybuses in October 1935. Poppy was then sent for scrap.

98. Car 350 looks quite sleek from this angle as it waits in Hanwell Depot yard. Note the original Brush built maximum traction trucks; each truck had a 50 hp motor. These trucks were later taken for use under car 330 (qv), and a replacement set was fabricated at Hendon Works. (H.Nicol)

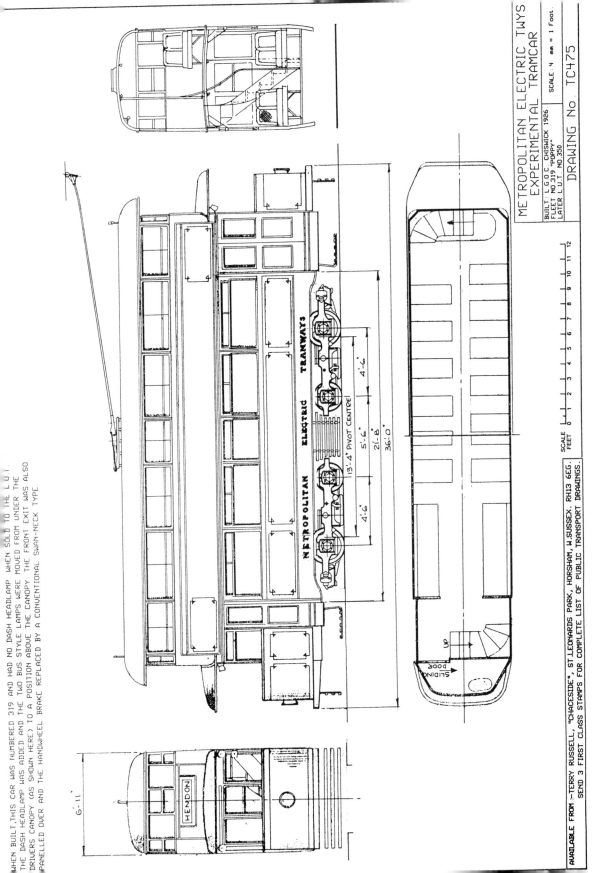

WHEN BUILT, THIS CAR WAS NUMBERED 319 AND HAD NO DASH HEADLAMP WHEN SOLD TO THE L.U.T.
THE DASH HEADLAMP WAS ADDED AND THE TWO BUS STYLE LAMPS WERE MOVED FROM UNDER THE
DRIVERS CANOPY (AS SHOWN HERE) TO A POSITION ABOVE THE CANOPY THE FRONT EXIT WAS ALSO
PANELLED OVER AND THE HANDWHEEL BRAKE REPLACED BY A CONVENTIONAL SWAN-NECK TYPE

METROPOLITAN ELECTRIC TRAMWAYS

HENDON

13'-4" PIVOT CENTRE
4'-6"
5'-6"
21'-8"
36'-0"
4'-6"

6'-11"

SLIDING DOOR
UP

METROPOLITAN ELECTRIC TWYS
EXPERIMENTAL TRAMCAR
SCALE 4 mm = 1 Foot.

BUILT L.G.O.C. CHISWICK 1926
FLEET NO.319 "POPPY"
LATER L.U.T. NO.350

DRAWING No. TC475

SCALE FEET 0 1 2 3 4 5 6 7 8 9 10 11 12

AVAILABLE FROM :- TERRY RUSSELL, "CHACESIDE", ST LEONARDS PARK, HORSHAM, W.SUSSEX. RH13 6EG.
SEND 3 FIRST CLASS STAMPS FOR COMPLETE LIST OF PUBLIC TRANSPORT DRAWINGS.

99. The upper deck accommodated 36 passengers on very comfortable, deep sprung seats covered in grey-green moquette. Unfortunately the ribs supporting the roof have not been concealed and this rather detracts from the overall appearance. (MET)

100. Since the car was equipped with platform doors, there was no need for bulkhead doors to cut out draughts. Here we look past the two-and-two seats which were rotated by the conductor when the car reversed at termini. (MET)

101. Car 320 is seen in all its splendour whilst on test at Golders Green. Notice the very modern shape of this tram, indeed the whole effect was nothing less than revolutionary, bearing in mind the traditional design that Londoners had come to expect from their tramcars. (H.Nicol)

MET car 320 "Blossom".

After the experience gained with Bluebell and Poppy, a trio of new tramcars was ordered from the Union Construction Company of Feltham in Middlesex. The first of these vehicles, Blossom, arrived in 1929. It was a fully enclosed, lightweight car mounted on two equal wheel trucks; each truck had two 35 hp motors. As with car 318 a "passenger flow" design was employed which involved a separate entrance and exit doorway. The front exits were operated directly by the motorman. Again the Whetstone - Cricklewood service was chosen for trial runs, which meant that Blossom was based at Finchley Depot. This car was renumbered 2166 by LT and was broken up at Charlton Works early in 1937.

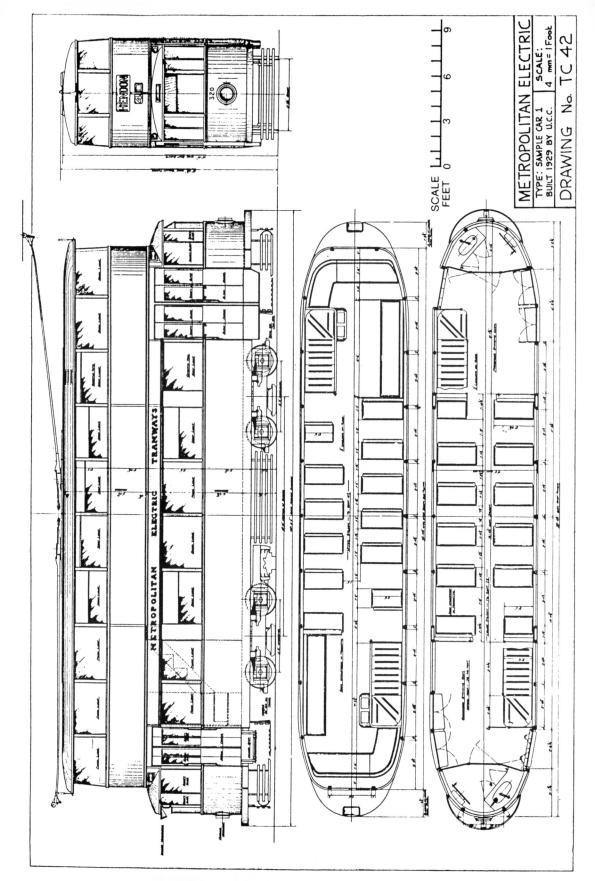

HENDON

320

METROPOLITAN ELECTRIC TRAMWAYS

SCALE FEET 0 3 6 9

METROPOLITAN ELECTRIC

TYPE: SAMPLE CAR 1
BUILT 1929 BY U.C.C.

SCALE:
4 mm = 1 Foot

DRAWING No. TC 42

102. Forty passengers could be transported in comfort on these luxurious seats. The upper deck panelling was covered with blue rexine and most of the metal fittings were chromium plated. (MET)

MET car 330.

This experimental tram was very similar to car 320 and it entered service on 6th November 1929. The livery was the standard MET vermilion, but the fleet name METROPOLITAN in gold lettering was carried on the side of the car. Like its predecessors car 330 spent its time allocated to Finchley Depot, and was renumbered 2167 by London Transport. It was transferred in August 1936 to Wood Green Depot and from there on 8th May 1938 it travelled south to Telford Avenue, Streatham where it ran on various South London routes. The end came in December 1949 when car 2167 was broken up in Purley Depot.

103. Cars 320 and 330 looked very similar, however, car 330 depicted here was equipped with maximum traction trucks removed from car 319. Also apparent in this view is the plough carrier next to the dog gate, this would enable the car to work over LCC conduit lines. (MET)

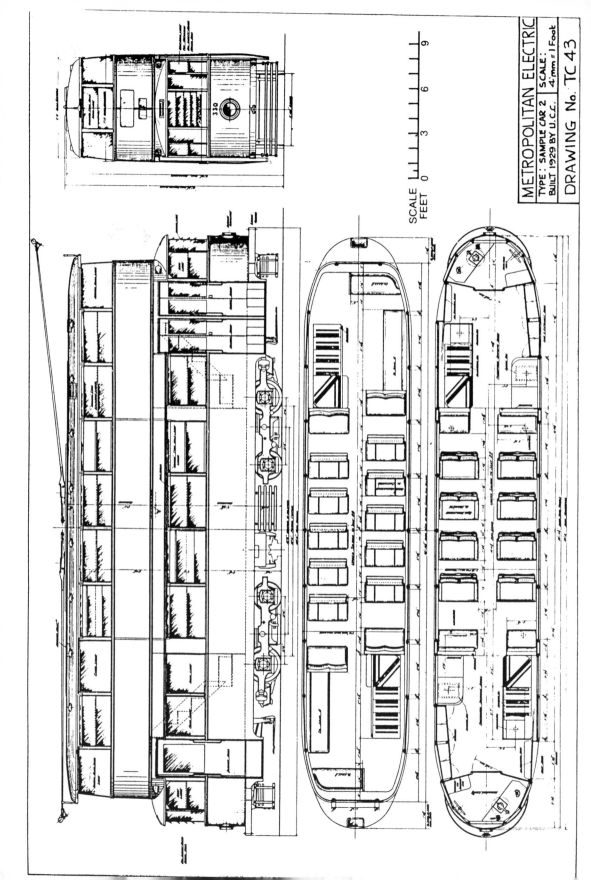

METROPOLITAN ELECTRIC

TYPE: SAMPLE CAR 2
BUILT 1929 BY U.C.C.

SCALE: 4 mm = 1 Foot

DRAWING No. TC 43

SCALE
FEET

0   3   6   9

MET car 331 "Cissie".

Perhaps the most attractive car of the trio was Cissie which was completed in December 1930 as a centre entrance car running on equal wheel bogies. Car 331 acted as a test vehicle for evaluating the response of the travelling public to boarding and alighting via a centre entrance/exit. London Transport renumbered the car 2168, but the centre entrance experiment was not particularly successful, thereby prompting an off-the-cuff remark by an LT official that the car would be better off working along Blackpool seafront, where this design was all the rage! The car was in fact sold in 1937 and it ended up on the northeast coast at Sunderland. Tentative enquiries for this unique vehicle were also received from Leeds and Aberdeen - one wonders what 331 would have looked like in dark blue livery on reserved tracks to Temple Newsam, or in dark green livery making its way through the granite city to Bridge of Don? One can only speculate on what might have been. The reality was that Cissie served out her time in Sunderland until the system closed in 1954. The car was then purchased by the late J.W.Fowler and can now be seen at the National Tramway Museum, Crich, Derbyshire.

104. A novel feature of car 330 was the provision for a seated conductor just below the PAY HERE sign. This system was soon given up, as delays in loading soon caused the conductor to resume his traditional, time honoured "roving" role to gather in all the fares. (MET)

105. In the author's opinion car 331 was and still is one of the most attractive double deck trams ever built; this broadside view accentuates the vehicle's sleek lines. The picture was taken before the car entered revenue service. (MET)

106. The most recent photograph in this book shows car 331 outside the main depot at the National Tramway Museum. One can only admire the superb restoration skills which have brought this vehicle back to life. (R.J.Harley)

TRACK CONSTRUCTION AND MAINTENANCE

107. In horse tram days it really was hard work! Here the construction crew takes a well earned rest, whilst the photographer records the scene for posterity. Note the heavy sections of girder rail required for electrification, and the piles of granite setts (cobbles) which all had to be sorted and positioned by hand. These "navvies" employed by a contractor on behalf of the London County Council Tramways, are seen digging up the road at Islington Green. (J.B.Gent Coll.)

The construction of tramways was traditionally very labour intensive. Most tasks associated with highway maintenance involved manual work with the help of rudementary tools such as picks and shovels. Only after electric tramways were an accepted part of urban life did the job improve by the gradual introduction of mechanical aids to lift and position rails and to grade the trackbed. The following photos give some idea of the hard work of the permanent way (PW) department. I dedicate this section to all those unsung heroes of the past who made sure that tramway travel was safe and reliable.

108. We have advanced to the year 1932, but the flat cap is still much in evidence as these track workers tackle a spot of trouble in Caledonian Road. Note the gas powered light which illuminates their probings at this section of pointwork. A single red oil lamp behind the chap with the spade was obviously considered sufficient in those days to warn oncoming motorists! (H.Nicol)

109. After the Second World War conditions for the PW staff improved somewhat, and the work of specialist outfits based at Rye Lane Depot was featured in an article in the London Transport Magazine. Training in the PW school took two weeks and then the newly trained trackmen, welders and pavers were sent out under supervision to tackle the backlog of work. In this picture a hut and a brazier serve to keep out the cold as the conduit tracks along Victoria Embankment are attended to. (J.C.Gillham)

110. Unlike today when yellow lines abound to prevent parking, in the early post-war years you could still dump a load of rails next to the pavement and not incur the wrath of shoppers and countless other statutory authorities! Here in South London rails wait to be renewed, and when night falls, there will be plenty of activity to get everything sorted out before the first tramcar in the morning. (A.J.Watkins)

111. The last entirely new route in London (before the present Croydon Tramlink) was the LCC's Westhorne Avenue extension opened in 1931/2. A mobile generator fitted to a PW department lorry supplies the power for the arc welding in the foreground, whilst girder rails and tie bars are in place waiting for the concrete gang to supply a firm track bed. A notice warns passers by about possible eyesight damage. (H.Nicol)

112. This contraption was an electrically powered machine whose function was to the grind rail joints after they had been welded, thus saving many man hours. It was also useful in tackling the nuisance caused by rail corrugation or "roaring rails", whereby the rail surface became pitted and subject to uneven wear. This caused noise problems and affected the smooth ride of the tramcars. (B.J.Cross Coll.)

113. Into the 1930s now, and although the trams were officially on their way out, this reconstruction of the Blue House railway bridge at Mitcham Common could wait no longer. In October 1936 a tram on service 30 crests the temporary bridge, whilst pedestrians make their way past track laid on wooden sleepers. It can easily be seen in the new road formation where the tram rails will be laid. Unfortunately this track had a very short life, as trolleybuses took over this section in September 1937. (H.F.Wheeller/R.S.Carpenter Coll.)

114. We observe track relaying in the final years of the system as more mechanical aids and better working conditions eliminated the need for large gangs of manual labourers. Indeed, here on Eltham Road, there doesn't seem to be a soul about! The red and white TRACK UP signs act as a warning for other traffic. (A.J.Watkins)

115. The swan song of the PW department happened with the construction of the new tramway roundabout in connection with the 1951 Festival of Britain. On Westminster Bridge Road by Stangate we again encounter car 186 which has just journeyed south from Highgate. On this misty day in December 1950 the pneumatic drills are quiet, since the job of constructing new conduit points is now almost complete. (J.H.Meredith)

FINALE

The end of this book seems an appropriate place to consider the last days of the trams in Barnet and Finchley. Briefly, they were removed in two stages: 2nd August 1936, all routes west of Finchley Depot. 6th March 1938, the final closure of local lines. The event in March 1938 attracted the attention of *Pennyfare*, the London Transport staff magazine, which ran an article entitled "Trolleybuses in the City - North London's Trams Almost Gone". The tone of the piece is, as one might expect, very pro-trolleybus, but the trams get an honourable mention. The article ends with a description of the last car from Barnet to Tally Ho Corner. We are told that Driver W.Lowe and Conductor F.Mardell who took the first tram to Barnet in 1907 also had the dubious privilege of closing the era on the last car.

116. The "end of the line", quite literally in this case, as rails are removed from East Street, Barking in April 1952. Sections of rail will then be cut up on site and loaded into lorries to be carted away for scrap. In parts of London many miles of track still lie dormant under several layers of tarmac. (J.H.Meredith)

117. The chap on the tower wagon ascends aloft as he installs spacer bar hangers for the new trolleybus overhead. Tram crews at North Finchley had to keep a wary eye open for these antics, as several minor accidents had already been reported; it was rumoured that some dyed-in-the-wool tram men had sabotage on their minds! (D.Jones Coll.)

118. In the distance, near Woodhouse Road, one of the new silver-roofed trolleybuses glides away, whilst two more traditional looking tramcars rumble along Kingsway. No doubt the motorman of the open fronted tram on route 9 was looking forward to a nice cab and a *driver's seat* in his new trolleybus. (R.J.Harley Coll.)

119. We look into the Nether Street tram station and realise that the trackless invaders have almost taken over. Trolleybus CGF 174 is obviously on a training mission in advance of the big day when North Finchley trolleybus station achieves its full potential. This status only lasted until 1961/2, when traffic pollution came to the area in a big way - in the shape of the Routemaster diesel bus! (A.J.Watkins Coll.)

120. Here at Fairfield Road, Barnet, one of the successors to the trams still supplies environmentally friendly transport, but not for much longer. The jet age, as typified by the BEA Comet 4B poster, seemingly only has time for the internal combustion engine, and as we are all well aware, the years since the 1960s have seen a rise of congestion and pollution in London to unacceptable levels. The long suffering public awaits a solution! (C.Carter)

MP Middleton Press

Easebourne Lane, Midhurst. West Sussex. GU29 9AZ   Tel: 01730 813169   Fax: 01730 812601

. . . . . Write or telephone for our latest list . . . . .

BRANCH LINES
Branch Line to Allhallows
Branch Lines to Alton
Branch Lines around Ascot
Branch line to Ashburton
Branch Lines around Bodmin
Branch Line to Bude
Branch Lines around Canterbury
Branch Line to Cheddar
Branch Lines to East Grinstead
Branch Lines around Effingham Jn
Branch Line to Fairford
Branch Line to Hawkhurst
Branch Lines to Longmoor
Branch Line to Lyme Regis
Branch Line to Lynton
Branch Lines around Midhurst
Branch Line to Minehead
Branch Lines to Newport
Branch Line to Padstow
Branch Lines around Portmadoc 1923-46
Branch Lines around Porthmadog 1954-94
Branch Lines to Seaton & Sidmouth
Branch Line to Selsey
Branch Lines around Sheerness
Branch Line to Southwold
Branch Line to Swanage
Branch Lines to Torrington
Branch Lines to Tunbridge Wells
Branch Line to Upwell
Branch Lines around Weymouth

LONDON SUBURBAN RAILWAYS
Caterham and Tattenham Corner
Clapham Jn. to Beckenham Jn.
Crystal Palace and Catford Loop
East London Line
Holborn Viaduct to Lewisham
Lines aound Wimbledon
London Bridge to Addiscombe
Mitcham Junction Lines
South London Line
West Croydon to Epsom
West London Line
Willesden Junction to Richmond
Wimbledon to Epsom

STEAMING THROUGH
Steaming through Cornwall
Steaming through East Sussex
Steaming through the Isle of Wight
Steaming through West Hants
Steaming through West Sussex

GREAT RAILWAY ERAS
Ashford from Steam to Eurostar
Festiniog in the Fifties
Festiniog in the Sixties

COUNTRY BOOK
Brickmaking in Sussex

SOUTH COAST RAILWAYS
Ashford to Dover
Bournemouth to Weymouth
Brighton to Eastbourne
Chichester to Portsmouth
Dover to Ramsgate
Ryde to Ventnor
Worthing to Chichester

SOUTHERN MAIN LINES
Bromley South to Rochester
Charing Cross to Orpington
Crawley to Littlehampton
Dartford to Sittingbourne
East Croydon to Three Bridges
Epsom to Horsham
Exeter to Barnstaple
Exeter to Tavistock
Faversham to Dover
Haywards Heath to Seaford
London Bridge to East Croydon
Orpington to Tonbridge
Sittingbourne to Ramsgate
Swanley to Ashford
Tavistock to Plymouth
Victoria to Bromley South
Waterloo to Windsor
Woking to Portsmouth
Woking to Southampton
Yeovil to Exeter

COUNTRY RAILWAY ROUTES
Bath to Evercreech Junction
Bournemouth to Evercreech Jn
Burnham to Evercreech Junction
Croydon to East Grinstead
East Kent Light Railway
Fareham to Salisbury
Frome to Bristol
Guildford to Redhill
Porthmadog to Blaenau
Reading to Basingstoke
Reading to Guildford
Redhill to Ashford
Salisbury to Westbury
Strood to Paddock Wood
Taunton to Barnstaple
Westbury to Bath
Woking to Alton

TROLLEYBUS CLASSICS
Croydon's Trolleybuses
Hastings Trolleybuses
Woolwich & Dartford Trolleybuses

TRAMWAY CLASSICS
Aldgate & Stepney Tramways
Bath Tramways
Barnet & Finchley Tramways
Bournemouth & Poole Tramways
Brighton's Tramways
Bristol's Tramways
Camberwell & W. Norwood Tramways
Croydon's Tramways
Dover's Tramways
East Ham & West Ham Tramways
Eltham & Woolwich Tramways
Embankment & Waterloo Tramways
Exeter & Taunton Tramways
Greenwich & Dartford Tramways
Hampstead & Highgate Tramways
Hastings Tramways
Holborn & Finsbury Tramways
Ilford & Barking Tramways
Kingston & Wimbledon Tramways
Lewisham & Catford Tramways
Maidstone & Chatham Tramways
North Kent Tramways
Portsmouth's Tramways
Reading Tramways
Seaton & Eastbourne Tramways
Southampton Tramways
Southend-on-sea Tramways
Stamford Hill Tramways
Thanet's Tramways
Victoria & Lambeth Tramways
Walthamstow & Leyton Tramways
Wandsworth & Battersea Tramways

OTHER RAILWAY BOOKS
Garraway Father & Son
Industrial Railways of the South East
London Chatham & Dover Railway

MILITARY BOOKS
Battle over Portsmouth
Battle Over Sussex 1940
Blitz Over Sussex 1941-42
Bognor at War
Bombers over Sussex 1943-45
Military Defence of West Sussex
Secret Sussex Resistance

WATERWAY ALBUMS
Hampshire Waterways
Kent and East Sussex Waterways
London's Lost Route to the Sea
London to Portsmouth Waterway
Surrey Waterways

BUS BOOK
Eastbourne Bus Story

SOUTHERN RAILWAY ● VIDEO ●
War on the Line